About Auth

Kamlesh Vishwakarma is a seasoned professional in the field of online marketing, renowned for his extensive 24 years of experience and expertise in technology and social media. As an Amazon-verified Advertising Partner, he showcases his credibility and proficiency in online advertising. Kamlesh consistently demonstrates strategic thinking abilities, adeptly crafting compelling content, managing advertising campaigns, and fostering online communities. His adeptness in harnessing the power of Amazon ads translates into tangible and impactful results.

About Walmart Marketplace

Walmart Marketplace is an eCommerce platform that allows **third-party sellers** to list and sell their products on Walmart.com right alongside Walmart's own inventory. It's kind of like Amazon's third-party seller system, but with **Walmart's massive customer base** and brand trust behind it.

Why Sell on Walmart Marketplace?

- **Huge Reach**: Walmart.com gets **over 100 million unique visitors monthly**.
- **Less Competition**: Compared to Amazon, there are fewer third-party sellers.
- **Trust Factor**: Customers trust Walmart, which can lead to better conversion rates.
- **Omnichannel Potential**: Sell online, but with the possibility of getting into stores later.

Why Walmart? Understanding the Opportunity

Why Walmart?

1. **Global Leader in Retail**
   - Walmart is the **world's largest retailer**, with a massive global presence. Being part of such a successful and influential organization provides unique exposure to cutting-edge retail strategies, logistics, and technology.

2. **Career Growth Opportunities**
   - o Walmart offers **clear career advancement paths**—whether you're starting in a store, in supply chain, tech, or corporate roles, there are structured programs to help you grow within the company.
3. **Commitment to Innovation**
   - o Walmart is investing heavily in **digital transformation**, AI, automation, and e-commerce. For tech-savvy or business-minded individuals, this means you're part of a company that's constantly evolving.
4. **Customer and Community Focus**
   - o The company has a strong focus on **customer satisfaction** and **community impact**. Through sustainability initiatives, diversity and inclusion efforts, and local support, Walmart aims to make a positive difference.
5. **Learning Culture**
   - o With in-house development programs like **Walmart Academy**, employees are encouraged to upskill and take charge of their learning journey.

Understanding the Opportunity

1. **Impact at Scale**
   - o Working at Walmart means your ideas or work can impact **millions of customers** and **hundreds of thousands of employees**. That's a rare opportunity to make a difference on a large scale.
2. **Challenging, Fast-Paced Environment**
   - o You'll be tackling real-world challenges—whether in operations, supply chain, technology, or customer service—in a fast-moving industry.
3. **Cross-Functional Collaboration**

- Opportunities often involve **collaboration across departments and disciplines**, giving you a well-rounded perspective on business and operations.
4. **Global & Local Reach**
    - While Walmart is a global player, many roles also involve understanding and serving **local markets**, which adds layers of strategy and customer focus.
5. **Stability with Innovation**
    - Walmart combines the **stability of a Fortune 1 company** with the agility of a company that's reinventing retail. That balance can be attractive for long-term career planning.

Setting Up for Success: Creating Your Seller Account

Creating your Walmart Seller account involves several steps to ensure you're set up properly to sell on Walmart Marketplace. Here's a step-by-step guide to help you get started:

Step 1: Check Eligibility

Before you apply, make sure you meet Walmart's basic requirements:

- U.S. Business Tax ID (EIN) and W9/W8 form
- A U.S. business address
- A product catalog that meets Walmart's standards
- Fulfillment capability within the U.S.
- Prior eCommerce experience (preferable)

Step 2: Gather Required Documents

You'll need:

- EIN Verification Letter from the IRS
- A digital copy of your W9
- Bank account info for payments
- Company address & contact info
- Product information (categories, pricing, etc.)

Step 3: Apply to Sell on Walmart Marketplace

1. Visit Walmart Marketplace Application Page
2. Fill in details about your business:
   - Company name, tax ID
   - Operations and fulfillment details
   - Catalog and product types
3. Submit your application

Approval usually takes **a few days to a few weeks.**

Step 4: Set Up Your Seller Center Account

Once approved:

1. You'll receive a confirmation email with login credentials for **Walmart Seller Center**
2. Log in and complete your profile:
   - Business details
   - Shipping options
   - Return policies
   - Tax settings
3. Set up your **payment info** via **Hyperwallet**

Step 5: List Your Products

You can add products:

- Manually through the Seller Center
- In bulk using a spreadsheet
- Via API or approved third-party integrations (e.g., Shopify, ChannelAdvisor)

Make sure to:

- Use clear titles & descriptions
- Add high-quality images
- Ensure competitive pricing

Step 6: Go Live

After uploading your catalog and finalizing setup:

- Walmart will review your listings
- Once approved, your products will go live!

Get your product listed

Creating a listing on **Walmart Marketplace** involves a few key steps in the **Walmart Seller Center**. Here's a breakdown of how to do it, whether you're adding one product or uploading in bulk:

Step-by-Step: Creating a Product Listing

1. Log into Walmart Seller Center

Go to <u>Seller Center</u> and sign in with your credentials.

2. Navigate to "Add Items"

- In the top menu, go to:
  Products > Add Items

3. Choose Your Upload Method

You can list products in **three ways**:

Option 1: Add a Single Item (Manually)

- Choose "Add a Single Item"
- Enter product information:
  - Product ID (UPC, GTIN, or ISBN)
  - Product Name
  - Brand
  - Category
  - Description & Key Features
  - Images (high quality, white background)
  - Price
  - Shipping & Returns info
  - Inventory count

Option 2: Bulk Upload via Spreadsheet

- Choose "Add Items in Bulk"
- Download the correct **category-specific template**
- Fill it out in Excel:
  - Use accurate, clean data (no typos, match required format)

- Upload the file back into Seller Center
- Monitor status under Feed Status

Option 3: Integration/API (for advanced sellers)

- Use Walmart APIs or connect via integration tools like:
  - Shopify
  - ChannelAdvisor
  - Zentail
  - GeekSeller

4. Submit and Review

- Once submitted, Walmart will **review and process** the listings
- Listings may take **a few hours to a couple of days** to go live

Product Listings That Convert

Creating high-converting listings on Walmart Marketplace is all about clarity, keyword optimization, and trust signals. Here's how to craft listings that **rank higher, attract clicks, and drive purchases**:

1. Understand Walmart's Algorithm (WPA)

Walmart uses its **Walmart Product Algorithm (WPA)** to rank listings. It considers:

- **Product relevance** (keywords, category)
- **Price competitiveness**
- **Shipping speed**

- **In-stock status**
- **Seller performance** (ratings, return rates)

Your listing needs to be **complete, optimized, and competitive** to win visibility and the Buy Box.

2. Optimize the Product Title

Format: Brand + Key Features + Product Type + Size/Quantity (if relevant)

Example:
"Samsung 65-Inch Class 4K UHD Smart LED TV with HDR — Model UN65TU7000FXZA"

Tips:

- Use the most **important keywords** first
- Avoid ALL CAPS or symbols like "!!" or "***"
- Be concise and relevant

3. Use High-Quality Images

- **Main image:** White background, full product view
- Add **lifestyle images**, packaging shots, zoomed-in details
- **Image size:** Minimum 1000 x 1000 px (better zoom quality)

Walmart allows up to **9 images**—use them all if possible.

4. Write Clear, Persuasive Descriptions

Short Description (Key Features):

- Bullet points (3–10)

- Focus on top benefits, specs, and use cases
- Include keywords naturally

Long Description (Optional but powerful):

- Paragraph form or HTML (if allowed)
- Use storytelling, use cases, care instructions, warranties
- Reinforce trust and value

5. Add Backend Keywords & Attributes

Walmart uses structured data heavily:

- Fill in **as many product attributes** as possible (color, size, material, age range, etc.)
- Add backend **search terms (keywords)** where allowed

More filled-out data = better search results and category placement.

6. Competitive Pricing

- Use Walmart's **Price Competitiveness tool** in Seller Center
- Consider dynamic repricing tools
- If you can offer **free or 2-day shipping**, you're more likely to win the Buy Box

7. Fast, Reliable Fulfillment

- 2-day shipping = huge boost to conversion
- Consider **Walmart Fulfillment Services (WFS)** for Prime-like advantages
- Keep inventory updated—out-of-stock = lower rankings

8. Boost Credibility with Reviews

- Encourage post-purchase reviews via email (if compliant)
- Use tools like Bazaarvoice to syndicate reviews from other platforms
- Respond to negative reviews professionally

9. Test and Tweak

- Monitor conversion rates, impressions, and Buy Box wins
- Try A/B testing titles or images
- Optimize seasonally and for trends

Quick Checklist for High-Converting Listings:

- Clear, keyword-rich title
- At least 4–6 high-quality images
- Short bullet-pointed description with key features
- Long description with use cases or benefits
- Accurate attributes filled in
- Competitive price
- Fast shipping options enabled
- At least 3-5 reviews (ideally with images)
- Inventory always in stock

Pricing Strategies for Maximum Profit

Walmart Marketplace is **highly competitive**, but with the right pricing approach, you can maintain strong margins **without racing to the bottom**. Here's how:

1. Competitive but Strategic Pricing

Walmart's Buy Box favors **lowest price + fast shipping**, but that doesn't always mean cheapest wins.

Strategy:

- Price **slightly lower or equal** to top competitors
- Include **shipping costs** in total price (Walmart considers "landed price")
- Use **price bands**—set min/max prices that keep your margins safe

Tools to help:

- **Walmart Repricer** (inside Seller Center)
- Third-party tools like **Repricer.com, Informed.co, or SellerActive**

Pro Tip: Don't underprice too much. It kills your brand perception and may trigger MAP violations if you're working with manufacturers.

2. Dynamic Pricing (aka Smart Repricing)

Adjust your pricing automatically based on:

- Competitor prices
- Inventory levels
- Buy Box wins
- Time of day or demand

Use dynamic repricing when:

- Selling commodity or high-volume products
- Competing against multiple sellers for the same item
- Stock levels are high

3. Bundle Pricing for Value Perception

Instead of lowering prices, **increase perceived value**:

- Offer product bundles (e.g., phone + charger + case)
- Combine slow-moving items with best-sellers
- Use **multi-pack discounts**

Customers feel like they're getting more—and you move more inventory at a good margin.

Psychological Pricing

Walmart is a price-sensitive marketplace. Use techniques like:

- **Charm pricing:** $29.99 vs. $30.00
- **Tier pricing:** Offer 1 unit at $10, 3 units at $27
- **Anchor pricing:** Show MSRP next to your discount

Example:

MSRP: $59.99
Your Price: **$44.98**
Customers see savings without you slashing your profit.

5. Shipping-Inclusive Pricing

Customers LOVE free shipping—and Walmart rewards it.

Strategies:

- Include **shipping cost in your product price**
- Offer **free shipping thresholds** (e.g., "Free shipping on orders over $35")
- Use **Walmart Fulfillment Services (WFS)** to simplify shipping + win Buy Box more often

6. Use Promotions & Rollbacks (The Walmart Way)

- **"Rollback" pricing** mimics Walmart's in-store discounts
- **Sponsored product promos** + temporary markdowns can boost visibility and conversions
- Always monitor ROI: test promos, then scale what works

7. Monitor Profit Margins Religiously

Don't sacrifice profit just to compete.

Use this simple formula to stay profitable:

Profit = Selling Price − (Product Cost + Shipping + Fees + Ads)

Track metrics in **Seller Center** or tools like:

- **Helium 10 Profits**
- **DataSpark**
- **Walmart Analytics**

Walmart Pricing Success Checklist

- Price is competitive, but protects margin
- Fast/free shipping included or WFS enabled
- Dynamic repricing tool in place

- Product bundles or value packs used where possible
- Pricing psychology tactics (e.g. $X.99) applied
- Promotions or Rollbacks scheduled strategically
- Margins tracked and adjusted monthly

Winning the Buy Box

Winning the **Buy Box on Walmart** is **crucial** for increasing sales—it's where the majority of purchases happen. On Walmart Marketplace, only **one seller gets the Buy Box at a time**, and unlike Amazon, Walmart doesn't always default to the cheapest price. Here's how to give yourself the **best shot at winning it** consistently:

1. Price Competitively (But Not Recklessly)

Walmart uses **"Landed Price"** (product price + shipping) to evaluate who wins the Buy Box.

Tips:

- Keep pricing competitive but **within your margin**
- Use **automated repricers** to adjust dynamically
- Consider all-in-one pricing (free shipping included)

Pro Tip: The lowest price doesn't always win if shipping, stock, and performance are weak.

2. Offer Fast & Reliable Shipping

Walmart prioritizes sellers who can **deliver quickly and on time**.

Strategies:

- Enable **2-day shipping** or **next-day delivery**
- Use **Walmart Fulfillment Services (WFS)** to boost shipping speed & trust
- Always update tracking promptly

Sellers using WFS are more likely to win the Buy Box—even if their prices are slightly higher.

3. Keep Inventory in Stock

No stock = No Buy Box. Even a brief stockout can knock you out of rotation.

Checklist:

- Sync inventory across platforms
- Use safety stock buffers
- Get alerts for low inventory

4. Maintain High Seller Performance

Walmart closely watches your:

- **Order Defect Rate (ODR)**
- **On-Time Shipping Rate**
- **Customer response time**
- **Cancellation & refund rates**

Top-performing sellers with fast fulfillment and great reviews are prioritized.

5. Optimize Your Listings

A strong listing can improve your product rank and visibility, influencing Buy Box success.

Make sure you have:

- Accurate titles with relevant keywords
- High-quality images
- Competitive attributes (like size, color, material)
- Clear descriptions and policies

6. Use WFS (Walmart Fulfillment Services)

This is a major **Buy Box booster**.

Why?

- Products ship faster and more reliably
- Walmart favors WFS listings
- You'll automatically qualify for 2-day shipping badges

Sellers in WFS often win Buy Box **even if priced slightly higher**.

7. Encourage Positive Reviews

Social proof matters. While reviews don't directly *guarantee* Buy Box wins, they:

- Improve listing performance
- Boost customer trust
- Reduce returns & negative feedback

8. Monitor & Adjust Regularly

Use the **Walmart Seller Center > Buy Box report** to track:

- Which SKUs are winning
- Win rate over time
- Pricing or shipping issues

Stay on top of changes and tweak your strategy regularly.

Buy Box Optimization Summary:

Factor	Action Needed
Competitive Price	Use repricing tools; factor in shipping
Fast Shipping	Enable 2-day delivery or use WFS
Inventory	Keep stock updated in real-time
Seller Performance	Maintain low ODR, fast responses
Listing Quality	High-quality titles, images, and details
Reviews	Encourage and manage customer feedback

Managing Inventory like a Pro

Smooth inventory management isn't just about not running out—it's about **maximizing Buy Box wins, avoiding order issues**, and setting yourself up for growth.

1. Integrate an Inventory Management System (IMS)

Using Walmart Seller Center alone can work for small catalogs, but pros go bigger.

Top IMS tools:

- **Sellbrite** (Walmart's official partner)
- **ChannelAdvisor**
- **Cin7, Skubana, Linnworks**
- Or native integrations through **Shopify, BigCommerce, etc.**

Why it matters:

- Real-time sync across channels
- Prevent overselling or stockouts
- Easier forecasting & replenishment

Tip: Choose a system that supports multichannel if you're also on Amazon, eBay, or Shopify.

2. Set Inventory Buffers

Walmart penalizes sellers for cancellations due to stockouts. Avoid that with safety stock.

Pro setup:

- Set a buffer (e.g., show 20 units when you have 25)
- Increase buffer during sales or peak seasons
- Use automatic rules in your IMS

A 5–10% buffer is usually safe, depending on your sales velocity.

3. Forecast Like a Boss

Look at **historical data, seasonality, trends, and sales velocity** to predict demand.

Forecasting tips:

- Track weekly/monthly sell-through rates
- Use Walmart analytics dashboards
- Monitor marketing events (like Walmart Rollbacks or ad campaigns)

Inventory = cash. Smart forecasting helps prevent both **overstocking** and **stockouts**.

4. Master Your Fulfillment Strategy

Your inventory setup depends heavily on how you fulfill orders:

Fulfilled by You (FBM):

- Keep stock updated across all warehouses
- Use fast, trackable shipping carriers
- Consider regional fulfillment to reduce delivery times

Walmart Fulfillment Services (WFS):

- Ship inventory in bulk to WFS centers
- Let Walmart handle storage, picking, packing, and shipping
- Real-time WFS inventory is auto-synced to your listings

WFS = fewer headaches and higher Buy Box potential.

5. Set Reorder Points & Automate Restocking

Reordering at the right time = steady cash flow + happy customers.

Pro tip: Use the formula

Reorder Point = (Avg. Daily Sales × Lead Time in Days) + Buffer Stock

Automate reminders or POs (purchase orders) through your IMS or supplier dashboard.

6. Monitor Inventory Health

Keep tabs on these metrics regularly:

- **Aging inventory** (dead stock = dead money)
- **Low inventory alerts**
- **Backorder rates**
- **Inventory turnover ratio**

Aim for high turnover, low obsolescence, and fast-moving SKUs.

7. Walmart Inventory Best Practices Checklist

Task	Frequency	Tool/Notes
Sync stock across channels	Daily	IMS or direct API
Monitor low stock alerts	Daily	IMS or Seller Center
Forecast sales trends	Monthly	Walmart Analytics
Replenish top SKUs	Weekly/Biweekly	Reorder automation
Remove old/stale stock	Monthly	Discounts or bundles
Review WFS storage fees	Monthly	WFS dashboard

Bonus Moves:

- Use **custom SKU labeling** for faster warehouse handling

- Consider **split inventory** between FBM + WFS for flexibility
- Add a **"back-in-stock" notification** for fast-selling items if you're on D2C too

Shipping & Fulfillment Options: WFS vs. FBM

Walmart offers two primary fulfillment methods for Marketplace sellers:

- **WFS** = Walmart Fulfillment Services (Walmart stores and ships your products)
- **FBM** = Fulfilled by Merchant (you handle storage, shipping, and customer service)

Each has pros and cons—here's how they stack up

1. Walmart Fulfillment Services (WFS)

WFS is **Walmart's in-house version of FBA (Fulfillment by Amazon)**. You send your inventory to Walmart warehouses, and they take care of the rest.

Benefits:

- **2-Day Shipping Badge** = major boost in visibility + Buy Box chances
- **Higher conversion rates**
- Walmart handles:
  - **Storage**

- o **Picking & packing**
- o **Shipping & tracking**
- o **Returns**
- o **Customer service**

Costs:

- Storage fees (monthly)
- Fulfillment fees (per unit, based on weight/dimensions)
- No setup or subscription fees

▢ Ideal For:

- Sellers who want Prime-like speed without the overhead
- High-volume or fast-moving SKUs
- Sellers focused on **Buy Box wins** and hands-off logistics

2. Fulfilled by Merchant (FBM)

FBM means **you manage your own inventory and shipping** (via your warehouse, 3PL, or home office).

Benefits:

- **More control** over inventory and logistics
- No fulfillment/storage fees to Walmart
- Easier to manage bundles or custom packaging
- Great for oversized, seasonal, or niche items

Challenges:

- You must offer **competitive shipping speeds** (ideally 2-day)
- You're responsible for:
  - o On-time delivery

- o Tracking uploads
- o Handling returns & customer inquiries
- Lower Buy Box odds if shipping is slow

Ideal For:

- Sellers with existing warehouse/3PL infrastructure
- Unique, made-to-order, or slow-moving inventory
- Sellers wanting tighter control over branding or packaging

WFS vs. FBM: Side-by-Side

Feature	WFS	FBM
Buy Box Advantage	Strong	Weaker unless shipping is fast
2-Day Shipping Badge	Included (WFS exclusive)	Must qualify manually
Storage & Fulfillment	Handled by Walmart	Seller's responsibility
Customer Service	Walmart handles it all	You handle every ticket
Fees	Storage + fulfillment per unit	Your own shipping & labor costs
Scalability	Easy to scale fast	Depends on your operations

How to Choose?

Ask yourself:

- Do I want to scale fast with minimal hands-on work? → **Go WFS**
- Do I already have a great 3PL or want full control? → **Stick with FBM**
- Can I ship 2-day reliably on my own? If not, **WFS wins on conversion & visibility**

Many top sellers use a hybrid model—WFS for fast-moving items, FBM for niche or slower SKUs.

Advertising on Walmart: Boosting Visibility

Why Advertise on Walmart?

- Walmart.com sees **over 120 million monthly visitors**
- Organic visibility takes time; **ads give you instant shelf space**
- Helps with **product launches, seasonal pushes**, and **competitive categories**

Types of Walmart Ads (via Walmart Connect)

1. Sponsored Products *(Most Popular)*

Promote individual products **within search results, carousel placements**, and **product detail pages**.

- Pay-per-click (PPC) model
- Target by **keywords or automatic placements**
- Great for **launching new listings** or **boosting best sellers**

Best For: Direct visibility + driving sales

2. Search Brand Amplifier (SBA)

Boost your **brand banner** at the top of search results with:

- Brand logo
- Custom headline
- Up to 3 featured products

Best For: **Brand awareness** and multi-product exposure

*Requirements: Need to be a **brand-registered** seller*

3. Display Ads *(Advanced)*

Showcase your brand or products **across Walmart's website, app, and off-site partners.**

- Can retarget past visitors
- Available via **Walmart DSP (Demand-Side Platform)**

Best For: High-budget campaigns, **retargeting**, and **broad brand exposure**

Walmart Ad Targeting Options

Type	What It Does	Best For
Automatic	Walmart AI chooses where to place your ads	Beginners, testing, fast setup
Manual	You choose exact **keywords, match types**	Keyword-level control & optimization
Category	Targets customers browsing similar categories	Broad targeting across interest groups
Retargeting	Reach shoppers who viewed but didn't purchase	Cart abandonment, reminding interested buyers

Budgeting & Bidding Tips

- Start with **$50–$100 per day** for testing
- Use **Cost-per-click (CPC) strategy** to control spending
- Optimize bids by:
    - Lowering for non-converting keywords
    - Raising bids for high-ROAS performers
- Focus on **products with strong listings + good reviews**—ads work best with optimized pages

Optimize Your Ad Performance

1. **Track key metrics:**
    - Impressions
    - Click-through rate (CTR)

- o Conversion rate
- o ROAS (Return on Ad Spend)
2. **A/B test:**
   - o Try different keyword sets or product images
   - o Test automatic vs. manual campaigns
3. **Use Walmart Analytics tools** or 3rd-party platforms like:
   - o **Pacvue**
   - o **Teikametrics**
   - o **Perpetua**

Pro Tips for High-Performance Walmart Ads

- Always advertise products that are **Buy Box eligible**
- Use **strong keywords** in your listings to align with ads
- Start with **automatic targeting**, then **refine manually** over time
- Keep your **listing images and titles conversion-optimized** (ads bring traffic—your listing has to close the sale)

What to Do

- Launch auto Sponsored Products (7–14 days)
- Analyze data (top keywords, high CTR products)
- Create manual campaigns using top-performing keywords
- Layer in brand ads (SBA) if applicable
- Adjust bids weekly, pause underperformers

Campaign Types and When to Use Them

Walmart's advertising ecosystem is designed to help sellers reach high-intent shoppers right where purchase decisions are made — at the point of search and discovery. Understanding the different campaign types available is crucial for deploying an ad strategy that's both cost-effective and growth-driven.

Let's break down the core campaign types on Walmart and explore **when and why** to use each.

1 Sponsored Search Ads

Automatic Campaigns

What They Are:
In automatic campaigns, Walmart's algorithm determines which search queries and placements are most relevant for your products. You don't choose keywords or placements — Walmart does it for you.

Best For:

- **New sellers** just getting started with Walmart Ads.
- **Product launches** where keyword performance data is limited.
- **Broad reach and discovery** of new search terms.
- **Top-of-funnel awareness**.

Pros:

- Easy to set up.
- Walmart handles keyword targeting.
- Great for learning which terms convert.

Cons:

- Less control over targeting.
- Potential for wasted spend on irrelevant searches.

Pro Tip:
Use automatic campaigns to identify high-performing search terms, then move those into manual campaigns for tighter control and improved ROI.

Manual Campaigns

What They Are:
Manual campaigns allow you to select specific keywords or items you want to target. You can choose match types (broad, phrase, exact), set individual bids, and manage performance more directly.

Best For:

- **Experienced advertisers** seeking more control.
- **Campaign optimization and scaling.**
- **Brand and product defense** (e.g., targeting your own branded keywords).
- **Targeting high-intent or competitive search terms.**

Pros:

- Greater control over keywords and budget.
- Ability to bid differently on individual terms.
- Ideal for scaling profitable campaigns.

Cons:

- Requires keyword research and regular optimization.
- More time-consuming to manage.

Pro Tip:
Manually target branded, competitor, and high-converting keywords uncovered from automatic campaigns to drive focused traffic.

3. Item Group vs. Item-Level Targeting

Walmart lets you choose between **Item Group** and **Item-Level** targeting in both auto and manual campaigns.

Item Group Targeting

You bundle multiple related SKUs (e.g., same product in different sizes or colors) and advertise them as a group. Walmart decides which variation to show.

Best For:

- Products with multiple variations.
- Simplified campaign setup.

Item-Level Targeting

You target a specific SKU in your campaign.

Best For:

- Highlighting best-selling variations.
- Campaigns with specific sales goals (e.g., push one SKU hard).

4. Sponsored Brand Amplifier (if available)

Note: This feature may be available only to brand owners or select sellers.

What It Is:
Sponsored Brand Amplifier is a premium ad format that promotes your brand and a collection of products at the top of search results, similar to banner ads.

Best For:

- **Brand awareness** and credibility.
- **Showcasing product lines.**
- **Driving cross-sells.**

Pro Tip:
Use Sponsored Brand Amplifier during peak shopping periods or brand launches to create a strong visual presence.

When to Use Each Campaign Type (At a Glance)

Campaign Type	Best Use Case	Control Level	Ideal For
Automatic Campaign	Discovering new keywords, testing	Low	Beginners, product launches
Manual Campaign	Optimizing, scaling, brand defense	High	Experienced sellers
Item Group Targeting	Similar products, quick setup	Medium	Large catalogs, variation ads

Campaign Type	Best Use Case	Control Level	Ideal For
Item-Level Targeting	Specific product focus	High	Hero products, top performers
Sponsored Brand Ads	Brand-building, multi-product campaigns	High	Brand owners, awareness goals

2. Sponsored Brand Ads

Walmart Sponsored Brand Ads are a powerful advertising solution within Walmart Connect, the retail giant's advertising platform. These ads are designed to increase visibility and drive traffic to a curated selection of products, allowing brands to showcase their identity prominently on Walmart's digital properties, including Walmart.com and the Walmart app.

What Are Sponsored Brand Ads?

Sponsored Brand Ads appear in high-traffic areas of Walmart's online marketplace, such as search results and category pages. They feature custom creative elements, including:

- A brand logo
- A custom headline
- A selection of products (typically 2-4 SKUs)

These ads link to a Walmart Brand Page or a curated landing page, making them ideal for storytelling, promoting new launches, or driving deeper engagement with the brand.

Key Benefits

1. **Increased Brand Visibility**
   Sponsored Brand Ads help brands stand out at the top of search results or on category pages, enhancing discoverability and driving awareness.
2. **Stronger Brand Presence**
   These ads allow brands to control messaging and aesthetics, making it easier to create a consistent, recognizable presence across Walmart's platform.
3. **Higher Click-Through and Conversion Rates**
   By showcasing multiple products and a compelling value proposition, Sponsored Brand Ads can encourage more exploration and purchases.
4. **Custom Targeting Options**
   Walmart Connect uses proprietary first-party data to enable precise audience targeting based on intent, demographics, and purchase behavior.
5. **Measurable Results**
   Brands have access to robust reporting tools that provide insights into impressions, clicks, sales, and return on ad spend (ROAS).

How It Works

To launch a Sponsored Brand campaign, brands typically go through Walmart's self-serve ad platform or work with Walmart Connect's managed services team. The process includes selecting products to feature, crafting the creative (logo and headline), and setting a budget and bid strategy. Walmart's algorithm then determines ad placements based on relevancy and bidding.

Best Practices

- Feature top-selling or seasonally relevant products
- Use eye-catching logos and clear, benefit-focused headlines
- Regularly review performance data to optimize bids and targeting

3. Display Ads

Walmart Display Ads are a key component of the Walmart Connect advertising ecosystem, designed to help brands reach Walmart's vast customer base both on and off Walmart's digital properties. These visual, banner-style ads use Walmart's rich first-party data to deliver personalized, targeted messages that drive awareness, consideration, and conversion.

What Are Walmart Display Ads?

Walmart Display Ads are visually engaging advertisements that appear across various placements, including:

- **On-site**: Walmart.com, the Walmart app, product detail pages, search results, and homepage.
- **Off-site**: Third-party websites and apps, via Walmart's programmatic demand-side platform (DSP).
- **In-store**: Through digital screens within physical Walmart stores.

They come in a variety of formats such as banners, carousels, and native ad units, and can include rich media elements like videos or interactive features.

Key Benefits

1. **Full-Funnel Reach**
   Display Ads support brand goals across all stages of the shopper journey—from building awareness to retargeting and driving conversions.
2. **Advanced Audience Targeting**
   Walmart leverages its proprietary first-party shopper data to target ads based on actual purchase behavior, demographics, and intent signals.
3. **Cross-Channel Visibility**
   With the Walmart DSP, brands can serve display ads not just on Walmart properties, but across the open web, reaching customers wherever they browse.
4. **Closed-Loop Measurement**
   Walmart Display Ads are linked directly to in-store and online sales data, enabling advertisers to clearly see how campaigns impact performance and ROI.
5. **Custom Creative Solutions**
   Brands can develop dynamic, visually compelling ad creatives that align with seasonal campaigns, product launches, or promotional events.

Use Cases

- **New Product Launches**: Generate buzz with high-impact placements and wide reach.
- **Retargeting**: Re-engage shoppers who viewed but didn't purchase your product.
- **Brand Storytelling**: Highlight your brand's mission or unique selling points with rich visuals and narrative-driven formats.
- **Promotions & Deals**: Drive urgency and sales with limited-time offers and holiday campaigns.

Best Practices

- Use strong, clear imagery and concise messaging
- Align targeting with campaign goals—awareness vs. conversion
- Leverage A/B testing to optimize creatives and placements
- Monitor performance and adjust bids and audiences based on results

Conclusion

The key to campaign success on Walmart is knowing **when to use each campaign type** and how to transition strategically — starting with automatic for discovery, then shifting to manual for control and optimization. As you grow, layer in item-level targeting and brand ads for precision and visibility.

Next up, we'll dive deeper into keyword strategies and targeting techniques that pair perfectly with each campaign type.

Ad Campaigns Setup

Here's a simple breakdown for **Ad Campaigns Setup on Walmart Marketplace** using **Walmart Connect**:

How to Set Up Ad Campaigns on Walmart

1. Access Walmart Connect

- Go to: <u>Walmart Connect</u>
- Log in with your **Seller Center** credentials (or request access if you're new)

2. Choose Your Ad Type

Walmart offers a few ad formats:

- **Sponsored Products** (Most common & self-serve)
- **Sponsored Brands** (For brand awareness — requires brand registry)
- **Display Ads** (Managed through Walmart Connect team)

Start with **Sponsored Products** if you're new — they appear in search results & product pages.

3. Set Up a Sponsored Products Campaign

1. Go to your **Walmart Ad Center**
2. Click **Create Campaign**
3. Select:
   - **Manual** or **Automatic targeting**
     - *Auto:* Walmart matches your products with relevant searches
     - *Manual:* You choose specific keywords
4. Name your campaign

4. Set Budget & Bidding

- Choose **daily or lifetime budget**
- Set your **CPC (cost-per-click) bid**
  - Recommended: start low and adjust based on performance
- Choose campaign **start & end dates**

5. Select Products to Advertise

- Choose your SKUs from your Walmart catalog
- Make sure they are **in stock**, priced competitively, and have good images

6. Launch & Monitor

- Click **Launch Campaign**
- Use the **Ad Center dashboard** to monitor:
  - Impressions
  - Clicks
  - Spend
  - Sales
  - ROAS (Return on Ad Spend)

Pro Tips:

- **Start with Auto campaigns**, then analyze and switch to **Manual** with top-performing keywords
- Use **high-quality product titles and images**
- A/B test different bids and products
- Optimize listings *before* advertising

Keyword Strategy & Targeting Techniques

Walmart's advertising platform doesn't just reward spend—it rewards relevance. That means success lies in targeting the right keywords, aligning your ads with shopper intent, and constantly optimizing based on performance data. In this chapter, we'll break down how to build a winning keyword strategy and master the art of targeting.

1. Understanding Keyword Targeting on Walmart Ads

Unlike Amazon, Walmart's keyword targeting is a bit more streamlined—but no less powerful. With **manual Sponsored Products campaigns**, you have the ability to select specific keywords and choose how closely they must match a shopper's search query.

Walmart offers **three match types**:

- **Broad Match**:
  Your ad can appear when a shopper searches for a term that contains your keyword in any order, along with additional words.
  Example: Keyword = "wireless earbuds" → Can trigger for "best wireless earbuds for gym" or "bluetooth wireless earbuds".
- **Phrase Match**:
  Your ad appears when the shopper's query includes your keyword in the exact word order, possibly with extra words before or after.
  Example: Keyword = "wireless earbuds" → Can trigger for "buy wireless earbuds" but **not** "earbuds wireless".
- **Exact Match**:
  Your ad only shows when the search query matches your keyword exactly, or is a close variant (like plural/singular).
  Example: Keyword = "wireless earbuds" → Triggers for "wireless earbuds" and "wireless earbud".

2. Building a Solid Keyword List

Start with a combination of **broad discovery** and **precise intent targeting**. Here's a step-by-step approach:

Step 1: Research with Tools

Use tools like:

- **Walmart's Search Term Report** (from your automatic campaigns)
- **Helium 10**, **Jungle Scout**, or **DataHawk** (if they support Walmart)
- **Google Trends** and **Amazon keyword tools** (for crossover search intent)

Step 2: Create Keyword Tiers

Group your keywords into three categories:

- **High-converting core keywords** (Exact match)
- **Supporting long-tail phrases** (Phrase match)
- **Broad discovery terms** (Broad match)

Step 3: Prioritize by Intent

High-intent keywords like "buy", "best price", or product-specific terms (like model names) often convert better than generic search terms.

3. Targeting Techniques to Maximize ROI

A. Use Negative Keywords

Just like with other platforms, irrelevant traffic can eat your budget. Regularly review your reports and add **negative keywords** to prevent your ads from showing on low-converting or irrelevant queries.

Example: Selling premium headphones? Negative out "cheap," "replacement," or unrelated brands.

B. Keyword Harvesting from Auto Campaigns

Run **automatic campaigns** as "discovery engines." Analyze your search term reports weekly to identify:

- High-performing queries (move these to exact/phrase match in manual campaigns)
- Poor-performing queries (add as negatives)

C. Branded vs. Non-Branded Targeting

- **Branded Keywords**
  Target your own brand name to protect your turf from competitors. These usually have high ROAS.
- **Competitor Branded Terms**
  Carefully test targeting competitor brand names, but be cautious—clicks might be cheap, but conversions are lower if your product isn't directly comparable or better.
- **Generic Category Keywords**
  These bring broader exposure (e.g., "wireless headphones"), but monitor closely for efficiency.

4. Strategic Bid Adjustments

Don't bid the same amount for every keyword. Instead:

- Bid **higher on exact match high-converting keywords**
- Bid **moderate on phrase match for broader reach**
- Use **lower bids on broad match** for discovery and test

Also, adjust bids by device, time of day, or geography if the option is available and relevant to your product.

5. Monitor, Optimize, Repeat

Your keyword strategy isn't a one-and-done deal. Here's a regular optimization checklist:

- Review Search Term Reports weekly
- Add new high-performing keywords to manual campaigns
- Set poor-performing terms as negatives
- Adjust bids based on ROAS and CTR
- Test new keywords monthly
- Pause underperforming keywords after 2–3 weeks with no traction

Conclusion

A successful Walmart Ads keyword strategy is a blend of science and instinct. You need data to guide you—but also a deep understanding of your audience and product positioning. Use automatic campaigns to explore, manual campaigns to refine, and consistent optimization to scale.

Crafting High-Converting Ads

Running Walmart Ads is only part of the game—the real magic happens when your ads *convert*. That means your product listing, targeting, visuals, and pricing all work together to convince a shopper to click **and** buy. In this chapter, we break down the elements that go into crafting ads that *actually* convert.

1. Start with the Listing: Your Ad Foundation

Your **product listing** is what your Sponsored Product ad will showcase. If your listing isn't optimized, your ad performance will suffer—no matter how much you bid. Focus on the following elements:

A. Title Optimization

- Keep it **clear and keyword-rich**, but not spammy.
- Front-load the most important terms (brand, product type, key features).
- Follow Walmart's style guide to avoid suppression.

Example:
"Sony Wireless Noise-Canceling Headphones – Over-Ear Bluetooth Headset with Mic"

"Amazing High Quality Best Sounding Coolest Headphones"

B. Bullet Points & Descriptions

- Highlight key features, benefits, and use cases.

- Use scannable formatting: short bullets, emojis (if allowed), or bold feature terms.
- Be specific: replace "great sound" with "Dual 40mm drivers for deep bass and clear mids."

C. Images That Sell

- **Main Image** must be clean (white background, centered product).
- Add **lifestyle images** showing the product in use.
- Include **close-ups**, **packaging**, and **size context**.
- Use **infographics** to showcase specs and benefits.

Pro Tip: Use A/B testing (different images or titles) to see which version drives more conversions.

2. Competitive Pricing: Make the Click Count

Even with a great listing, shoppers bounce if your price isn't right.

- **Monitor your competitors** often, especially for similar listings.
- Use **Walmart's pricing tools** or third-party tools to stay competitive.
- Factor in shipping—**free shipping** often leads to higher conversion.

Pro Tip: Add temporary discounts or participate in Rollbacks to boost visibility and conversion during key periods.

3. Ratings & Reviews: Social Proof Sells

Walmart prominently displays ratings in ads. If you have **few or poor reviews**, conversion drops dramatically.

- Proactively ask customers for reviews post-purchase.
- Use the Walmart Review Accelerator (if available) to generate early feedback.
- Address negative reviews quickly and professionally.

4. Landing Page Consistency: Match Expectations

What a shopper **sees in the ad** should align perfectly with what they **find on the product page**. This builds trust and reduces bounce.

- If your ad shows a bundle or specific feature, make sure it's clearly shown and explained on the listing.
- Keep product titles consistent between your ad and landing page.

5. Use Item-Level Targeting for Best Sellers

Don't group your hero product with underperformers. Use **item-level targeting** in your campaigns to:

- Push your **top-selling SKUs** with high reviews and ratings.
- Control ad spend and bids more precisely.

6. Category & Search Term Relevance

Walmart's ad algorithm favors **relevant ads**. Even with a high bid, your ad won't show if the listing doesn't match the shopper's intent.

Make sure:

- Your **category** and **attributes** are correctly assigned in the listing backend.

- Your **keywords** are sprinkled naturally in the title, description, and bullet points.

7. Use Badges & Enhancements (if eligible)

Badges like:

- **Best Seller**
- **2-Day Delivery**
- **Pro Seller**
  ...can dramatically boost CTR and conversion.

Tip: Enroll in Walmart Fulfillment Services (WFS) to unlock fast shipping and increase badge eligibility.

8. A/B Testing: Small Tweaks, Big Impact

Test different elements to see what improves your conversion rate:

- Main image
- Product title
- Price point (e.g., $19.99 vs. $18.95)
- Bullet point structure

Track performance through Walmart Ad Reports and adjust based on data.

Conclusion

High-converting Walmart ads start with great product pages. Think of your ads as a spotlight—but what matters most is *what's in the spotlight*. Polish your listings, get your pricing right, and show shoppers why your product is worth clicking on—and buying.

Budget Allocation and Bid Optimization

Getting clicks is great—but getting **profitable** clicks is better. That's where budget allocation and bid optimization come into play. In this chapter, we'll walk you through how to structure your Walmart ad spend, allocate your budget effectively, and fine-tune your bids to maximize return on ad spend (ROAS).

1. Understanding Your Budgeting Options

Walmart Sponsored Products campaigns offer two main budgeting structures:

A. Daily Budget

The average amount you're willing to spend per day on a campaign.

Use when:

- You want **steady exposure** over time.
- You're running **always-on campaigns**.
- You want to avoid blowing your entire budget in a few hours.

B. Lifetime Budget

A total budget that runs over a set campaign duration.

Use when:

- You're running **time-bound promotions** (e.g., weekend sales, holiday events).
- You want **complete control** over your total spend.
- You're **testing new products or keywords**.

2. Budget Allocation Strategy: Prioritize Your Winners

Don't spread your budget thin across too many products. Instead, allocate based on:

Product Performance

Focus spend on:

- Top-selling items
- Highly rated products
- Listings with competitive pricing and strong reviews

Campaign Type

Start with:

- 60% for **manual campaigns** (for control and performance)
- 30% for **automatic campaigns** (for keyword discovery)
- 10% for **experimental/test campaigns**

Adjust based on results.

Funnel Stage

- **Top of Funnel** (awareness): Broad match, low bids, discovery focus
- **Middle of Funnel** (consideration): Phrase match, medium bids, branded keywords

- **Bottom of Funnel** (intent to purchase): Exact match, high bids, high-converting terms

3. Smart Bidding: The Art of Spending Wisely

Walmart uses a **first-price auction system**—meaning you pay what you bid. So every penny counts.

How to Approach Bidding:

Match Type	Starting Bid Strategy
Broad	Low to moderate ($0.30–$0.60)
Phrase	Medium ($0.50–$0.90)
Exact	Higher ($0.75–$1.50+)

Pro Tip: Monitor your campaign performance daily for the first week. Gradually raise bids on high-converting keywords, and reduce or pause those that burn budget without results.

4. Bid Optimization Tactics

Bid by Performance

- Raise bids on keywords with **high conversion rates** and strong ROAS.
- Lower bids or pause keywords with **high spend but low conversions**.

Adjust Bids Based on Product Margin

Don't overspend on low-margin products. Match your bid to what you can afford based on profit margin.

Device & Placement Adjustments (if available)

Some Walmart ad settings allow you to optimize for mobile vs desktop. Mobile typically has higher traffic—test and adjust accordingly.

5. Daily Optimization Checklist

Here's what to look at daily or weekly:

- **Impressions** – Are your ads being seen?
- **Spend** – Are you staying within budget?
- **Click-Through Rate (CTR)** – Is your targeting relevant?
- **Conversion Rate** – Are shoppers buying?
- **ROAS** – Are your ads profitable?

6. Scaling Your Budget

Once you find a winning product or keyword combo:

- **Increase your budget gradually** (10–20% every few days).
- Monitor metrics closely after each adjustment.
- Don't scale too fast—volume increases can tank ROAS if performance can't keep up.

7. Budget Saving Tips

- Use **dayparting** to schedule ads during peak times (if supported).

- Add **negative keywords** to prevent wasted spend.
- Focus on **exact match** for best ROAS control.
- Limit spend on **low-performing automatic campaigns**—harvest and shift to manual.

Conclusion

Walmart Ads isn't just about spending more—it's about spending smarter. By strategically allocating your budget and optimizing bids based on performance data, you'll squeeze more ROI out of every dollar. Always be testing, adjusting, and doubling down on what works.

Scaling Campaigns for Growth

Once you've dialed in your targeting, optimized your listings, and proven your ad campaigns are profitable, it's time to scale. But scaling isn't just about increasing your budget — it's about expanding reach strategically while maintaining efficiency. In this chapter, we'll explore how to grow your Walmart ad campaigns in a smart, sustainable way.

1. Confirm You're Ready to Scale

Before scaling any campaign, make sure it meets these criteria:

- **Consistent ROAS above your breakeven point**
- **Product listing is optimized** (images, reviews, title, description)
- **Sufficient stock and fulfillment capacity**

- **Proven keyword and campaign performance**

If you haven't nailed these yet — pause and optimize before scaling.

2. Scale Budget Slowly and Strategically

Walmart's ad algorithm doesn't always react well to sudden changes. A controlled increase keeps performance stable.

Budget Scaling Rule of Thumb:

- Increase daily budget **by 10–20% every 3–4 days**
- Monitor metrics like CTR, CPC, and ROAS after each increase

Avoid: Doubling your budget overnight — it usually leads to wasted spend before the algorithm adapts.

3. Expand Keyword Coverage

Once you've maxed out your current keyword targets:

- **Mine automatic campaign reports** for new high-performing terms
- Add **long-tail keywords** (e.g., "wireless earbuds for working out") to reach more specific shoppers
- Layer in **phrase and broad match** terms to attract wider intent while still staying relevant

Pro Tip: Segment keywords into tiers — invest more in exact match for best ROAS, and test new terms using lower bids in broad/phrase match.

4. Add More Campaign Types

Scaling isn't just about spending more on what's already working — it's also about **diversifying your campaign portfolio**.

Add More Manual Campaigns

Break out campaigns by:

- Product categories
- Keyword intent (e.g., branded, competitor, generic)
- Match type

Launch Sponsored Brand Ads (if eligible)

These can boost brand visibility and drive cross-selling opportunities.

Focus on High-Margin or Bundled Products

These give you more room to increase bids without hurting profit.

5. Segment by Product Performance

Create **tiered campaigns** based on product potential:

Tier	What It Includes	Budget Focus
Tier 1	Best sellers, high ROAS SKUs	60–70% of budget
Tier 2	Mid-performers	20–30% of budget
Tier 3	New or unproven products	10–20% (test zone)

Scale Tier 1 products first. Once performance stabilizes, promote strong Tier 2 performers.

6. Optimize for Conversion Rate

Scaling is pointless if your conversion rate drops. As you increase traffic, make sure your listings stay sharp:

- Keep pricing competitive
- Monitor review quality and volume
- Use A/B testing to improve product titles or imagery

7. Expand to New Keywords or Audiences

Explore opportunities like:

- **Targeting competitor brands** (carefully)
- **Seasonal keyword themes** (e.g., "back to school headphones")
- **Geographic targeting** (if available)

Diversify your ad exposure to reduce dependency on a single keyword or audience.

8. Monitor Closely and Optimize Relentlessly

Scaling without tight monitoring can tank your profitability. Watch for:

- Spiking CPCs
- Falling ROAS
- Decreasing CTR
- Ad fatigue (performance decline over time)

Use Walmart's reporting tools to spot issues early and course-correct fast.

9. Use Walmart Fulfillment Services (WFS)

Products fulfilled by Walmart often get priority in search rankings and win more Buy Boxes, which leads to higher conversions. If you're scaling, WFS can help:

- Improve delivery speed
- Qualify for 2-day shipping badge
- Increase visibility in ads and organic search

10. Set Scaling Milestones

Track your growth using metrics like:

- ROAS threshold (e.g., maintain 4.0+ while scaling)
- Daily spend target
- Revenue or unit sales goal
- Keyword expansion benchmarks

Scaling should feel intentional, not reactive.

Conclusion

Scaling your Walmart ad campaigns is about more than increasing your budget — it's about increasing your **impact**. Focus on optimizing what's working, expanding smartly into new areas, and keeping your conversion rate high as you grow.

Brand Store Front

Setting up a **Brand Storefront on Walmart** is a great way to create a fully branded shopping experience within Walmart.com. It allows you to showcase your products, highlight your brand story, and guide shoppers through a curated selection—all within your own customizable page.

How to Set Up a Brand Storefront on Walmart.com

*1. **Become a Walmart Marketplace Seller (If Not Already)***

Before creating a brand storefront, you must be an **approved seller** or **supplier** on the Walmart Marketplace.

2. *Enroll in Walmart Connect*

To build a brand storefront, you'll need access to **Walmart Connect**, Walmart's retail media platform. You can request access through your Walmart Seller Center or via your Walmart Connect rep if you're working with them directly.

3. Use the Walmart Brand Shop Tool

Once approved, you can build your storefront using the **Brand Shop Builder** inside Walmart Connect. It's a drag-and-drop tool for creating custom layouts and pages.

Key features:

- Custom banners and imagery
- Video content

- Product carousels
- Category navigation
- Storytelling sections (about the brand, sustainability, etc.)

4. Plan Your Page Layout

Typical Brand Storefront includes:

- **Hero banner** with your logo and tagline
- **Featured products**
- **Category navigation** (e.g., "Men's Shoes," "Summer Collection")
- **Brand story/about section**
- **Promotional modules** (sales, seasonal deals)

5. Upload Content & Build Pages

Use the builder to:

- Add high-resolution images and videos
- Create section headers
- Feature specific product groups (best sellers, new arrivals, etc.)
- Link directly to product pages or collections

Walmart allows you to build **multi-page storefronts**, not just a single landing page.

6. Submit for Review

Once your storefront is designed and populated, submit it for Walmart's approval. They'll review content for brand alignment, quality, and compliance.

7. Launch and Promote

Once approved, your Brand Storefront goes live on Walmart.com and can be accessed via:

- Sponsored Brand Ads
- Search placements
- Direct URLs
- Walmart event placements

You can now promote your storefront through **Walmart Connect ads**, social media, email, or influencer campaigns.

Pro Tips:

- Use high-quality lifestyle images to connect with customers
- Feature seasonally relevant products or collections
- Optimize your product detail pages to improve discoverability from your store
- Update your storefront regularly (holidays, launches, etc.)

Create a Shelf

Creating a **Shelf** on Walmart.com is a smart way to group and promote specific products under a unified theme. Shelves can help spotlight product collections like "Back to School," "Top Picks," or "New Arrivals," and are often used in conjunction with Walmart advertising like **Sponsored Brand Ads** or **Display Ads**.

How to Create a Shelf on Walmart.com

1. Be an Approved Walmart Seller or Supplier

To create a shelf, you must:

- Be a **registered seller** or **supplier** on Walmart Marketplace.
- Have access to **Walmart Connect** (Walmart's ad platform).

If you don't already have access, reach out to your Walmart Connect representative or request access via your Seller Center dashboard.

2. Use the Walmart Ad Center or Walmart Connect Portal

Shelves are typically created and managed through the **Walmart Ad Center** (for self-serve advertisers) or via **managed services** through Walmart Connect.

There, you'll find tools to:

- Create product collections
- Build ad campaigns
- Link those ads to your shelf

3. Build the Shelf Page

You'll need to submit a **Product ID list** (Item IDs or GTINs) for the products you want to feature.

Shelf Elements Include:

- Shelf Name (e.g., "Top Rated Kitchen Essentials")
- Short description or headline
- Product assortment (2–200+ SKUs)
- Optional custom banner image or background
- Landing URL: Walmart will generate a custom URL that directs to your shelf

These shelves are generally not part of your storefront, but they function as **mini curated landing pages**.

4. Use Shelf in Sponsored Ads

You can link your shelf to:

- **Sponsored Brand Ads** (showcase multiple products + drive to the shelf)
- **Display Ads** (targeted campaigns across Walmart and 3rd-party sites)
- **Seasonal Campaigns** (e.g., Black Friday, Summer Essentials)

This is where shelves shine—by acting as **campaign destinations** that convert better than single product listings.

5. Monitor and Optimize

Once live, you can track:

- Shelf traffic and product performance
- Click-through rates from associated ads
- Conversion rates and return on ad spend (ROAS)

You can update your shelf regularly—swap in new products, change banners, or realign with seasonal events.

Pro Tips:

- Group items with a common purpose or theme
- Use eye-catching shelf titles that speak to shopper intent (e.g., "Essentials Under $25")
- Ensure all product listings are optimized with images, reviews, and accurate pricing
- Promote your shelf across your own social media, email, or influencer content

Below the Fold Content (A+ Content)

Below the fold content on Walmart refers to the content that appears **lower on the product detail page (PDP)**—beneath the main images, title, price, and buy box. This section is prime real estate for **enhanced product content**, also known as **Rich Media** or **A+ Content** on Walmart.

Here's how you can get **below-the-fold content** live on your Walmart product pages:

1. Enroll in Walmart's Rich Media Program

Walmart doesn't allow every seller to directly upload enhanced content. You'll need to work with an **approved third-party Rich Media provider**, such as:

- **Salsify**
- **WhyteSpyder**
- **SKU Ninja + WhyteSpyder**
- **Bazaarvoice**

- **Content26**

These partners are authorized to publish below-the-fold content on Walmart.com.

2. Create Rich Media Content

This content enhances the product detail page and typically includes:

- Branded headers or banners
- Comparison charts
- Feature callouts
- Lifestyle imagery
- How-to videos or product demos
- FAQs or detailed specs

Think of it like a mini landing page **within the PDP**.

3. Submit the Content via a Rich Media Provider

Once your assets are designed:

- Your provider will upload and format them according to Walmart's guidelines
- They will assign the content to the appropriate **Item IDs (SKUs)**
- Walmart will then review and publish the content on the PDP

4. Monitor Performance

Below-the-fold content doesn't just look good—it often drives better outcomes:

- Higher conversion rates
- Longer time on page
- Fewer returns (thanks to better shopper understanding)

You can track performance via your **Seller Center** or analytics tools from your content provider.

Pro Tips:

- Keep content clean, visual, and mobile-friendly
- Use short, benefit-driven copy
- Show the product in real-life use cases
- Align content with your brand voice and Walmart's style guidelines

Seasonal & Promotional Campaign Tactics

Seasonal events and promotions are some of the most lucrative opportunities on Walmart.com. From Black Friday to back-to-school to summer sales, shoppers come ready to spend — but so does your competition. In this chapter, we'll break down how to prepare, execute, and optimize **seasonal and promotional campaigns** that drive high-volume sales and strong returns.

1. Understand the Power of Seasonality on Walmart

Walmart's platform sees huge traffic spikes during:

- **Holiday shopping** (Black Friday, Cyber Monday, Christmas)

- **Back-to-school season**
- **Valentine's Day, Mother's Day, Father's Day**
- **Summer travel & outdoor season**
- **Spring cleaning**
- **Walmart-specific events** (Rollbacks, seasonal promotions, clearance)

Why it matters:

Buyers during these windows often have **higher intent**, which can mean:

- Higher conversion rates
- Increased competition (CPCs rise)
- More opportunities to move inventory fast

2. Pre-Season Prep: Laying the Groundwork

You need to start **planning 4–6 weeks ahead** of any seasonal event. Here's what to do:

Optimize Listings Early

- Use **seasonal keywords** in your titles and descriptions (e.g., "gift for dad," "spring essentials").
- Add **seasonal lifestyle images** where appropriate.
- Ensure inventory is in place — and **WFS-enabled** if possible.

Identify Your Seasonal SKUs

Focus ad efforts on:

- Giftable items
- Seasonal must-haves
- High-margin bundles or limited-time products

Segment Campaigns by Season

Create dedicated **seasonal campaigns** to isolate budget and easily measure performance.

3. Promotional Tactics That Work

Use these tactics to boost visibility and conversions during peak periods:

Run Short-Term Manual Campaigns

- Use **exact and phrase match** with seasonal and holiday-related terms.
- Target **gift-buying behavior**: "gifts for dad," "holiday deals under $50," etc.

Leverage Rollbacks & Deals

Participating in Walmart deals helps your product appear with **"Rollback"** or **"Reduced Price"** badges — which can increase CTR significantly.

- Time your discounts with Walmart's promotional calendar
- Run ads **with higher bids** during promotional windows to gain visibility

Bundle & Promote

Create limited-time bundles that offer **value** and **urgency**:

- e.g., "Holiday Tech Gift Pack," "Winter Skincare Trio"

- Promote them via Sponsored Product campaigns and highlight the value in product titles

4. Increase Budgets Strategically

Expect **higher ad spend** during peak seasons — but plan for it.

- Increase budgets on your **top-performing products** and exact-match seasonal keywords
- Set a **lifetime budget** if you're running a campaign for a fixed period
- Start with 25–50% more daily budget 1–2 weeks before the seasonal spike

5. Boost Retargeting (if Available)

If you're using **Walmart Sponsored Display Ads** (or third-party DSP), seasonal periods are a great time to:

- Retarget recent viewers
- Push urgency messaging ("Ends Tonight!", "Final Day for Free Shipping")

6. Bid Aggressively — But Wisely

During major events like Black Friday, expect higher CPCs. To compete:

- **Prioritize exact-match high-intent seasonal keywords**
- Raise bids **gradually before the event**, not just on the day-of
- Monitor performance closely and **reduce bids quickly** on underperformers

7. Post-Season Opportunities

The party isn't over after the peak. Here's how to extend your results:

Clearance Campaigns

Push leftover inventory with **discounted pricing** and low-cost campaigns.

Analyze & Document

After every event:

- Pull keyword reports
- Note high-performing creatives and campaigns
- Document what worked (and what didn't) for next year

8. Real-World Campaign Example

Back-to-School Campaign (Example)
Products: Laptop, backpack, lunchbox
Timeline: July 15 – August 15
Prep: Listings updated, images show kids using products
Promo: "Back-to-School Bundle"

Ad Strategy:

- Broad match discovery 4 weeks before
- Phrase/exact match for "back to school laptop"
- Boost bids in last 10 days
- Use budget tiering: 60% on hero SKU, 30% on bundle, 10% on new products

Result: Higher CTR, strong ROAS on bundle, carry-over traffic into September

Promotions

Creating promotions on Walmart Marketplace is a great way for sellers to attract customers, increase sales, and boost product visibility. Walmart offers several ways to create promotional deals and special offers for your products. Below is an overview of how you can set up different types of deals.

Types of Promotions You Can Create on Walmart

1. **Discount Promotions:**
   - **Percent Off**: Offer a percentage discount on selected items (e.g., 10% off).
   - **Amount Off**: Provide a fixed amount off the original price (e.g., $5 off).
   - **Custom Price**: Set a custom promotional price for your product.
2. **Strikethrough Pricing:**
   - **Strikethrough Promotion**: This displays the original price with a line through it and shows the new discounted price, making it clear that customers are getting a deal.
   - The promotion must have a **Comparison Price** (like the "Was Price" or List Price) to qualify for the strikethrough.
   - For a strikethrough to appear, the promotional price must be at least **10% lower** than the Comparison Price.
3. **Clearance Sales:**

- Create special promotions for products you're clearing out. These items typically have deeper discounts, especially when inventory needs to be reduced quickly.
4. **Buy One, Get One (BOGO)**:
    - This deal allows you to offer a free item or a discount on a second item when a customer purchases one product. It's a great way to increase the average order value.
5. **Flash Sales**:
    - Flash sales are time-limited promotions that help create urgency. These deals often appear on Walmart's homepage, attracting a lot of traffic and potential customers.

Conclusion

Seasonal campaigns are your chance to hit revenue goals fast — but only if you plan ahead, optimize smartly, and act with urgency. From keyword tweaks to visual updates to strategic bidding, it all comes together during these critical windows.

Going Beyond — Building a Brand on Walmart

Walmart Marketplace isn't just a place to sell—it's a platform where you can **build a recognizable, trusted brand**. And in an environment full of low-cost competition, a strong brand helps you win the Buy Box, build customer loyalty, and grow long-term. In this chapter, we'll break down how to **strategically build your brand presence** on Walmart—from storefront to storytelling.

1. Why Brand Building Matters on Walmart

While Walmart is traditionally product-first, branding is becoming increasingly important for sellers who want to:

- Stand out from generic listings
- Create trust and recognition
- Increase repeat purchases
- Command premium pricing
- Drive success with Sponsored Brand Ads and enhanced content

2. Start with the Basics: Branding Through Your Product Listings

Your product pages are the **first impression** of your brand. Make sure they reflect your identity and quality:

Titles

- Keep titles clean, keyword-rich, and on-brand.
- Use consistent naming structures across SKUs.

Images

- Use **professional photos** with a branded, cohesive look.
- Include **lifestyle images** that reflect your brand values (eco, luxury, family-friendly, etc.).

Descriptions & Bullet Points

- Craft a brand voice: informative, playful, premium—whatever fits you.
- Emphasize your **unique value propositions** (ethically sourced, USA-made, lifetime warranty, etc.).

3. Create a Walmart Brand Storefront

Walmart allows **qualified sellers** to create a customizable brand storefront—think of it as your own branded mini-site.

Benefits:

- Showcase your full product catalog
- Organize by category, bestsellers, or promotions
- Reinforce brand visuals and messaging
- Improve shopper trust and navigation

Tips for a Strong Storefront:

- Use high-quality banner images with your logo and brand slogan
- Feature top-rated products and bestsellers
- Update for seasons or promotions (e.g., "Holiday Gift Picks")
- Include brand story sections ("Why Choose Us?")

4. Use Enhanced Content (A+ Content)

Walmart's **Rich Media Content** lets you go beyond basic product descriptions with:

- Image carousels
- Feature callouts

- Comparison charts
- Brand storytelling modules

Use this to:

- Build credibility
- Address common objections
- Differentiate your product from competitors

5. Leverage Walmart Sponsored Brands (if eligible)

Sponsored Brand Ads let you showcase your logo, custom headline, and featured products in premium placements.

When to use:

- For new product launches
- To promote bundles or collections
- During seasonal events or promos
- To drive traffic to your brand storefront

6. Build Loyalty Through Quality and Customer Experience

Branding isn't just visuals — it's **every touchpoint**. Build a reputation for quality by:

- Ensuring fast, reliable shipping (preferably with **Walmart Fulfillment Services**)
- Maintaining high product quality and consistency
- Responding to customer questions quickly
- Avoiding stockouts or order cancellations
- Encouraging reviews with follow-up messaging (where allowed)

Pro Tip: Over deliver on value — branded inserts, packaging, or thoughtful touches can turn one-time buyers into brand fans.

7. Collect and Showcase Social Proof

Positive reviews and customer feedback are powerful brand-builders.

- Request reviews post-purchase through follow-ups (if compliant with Walmart's policies)
- Highlight 4+ star products in Sponsored Brand Ads
- Use UGC (user-generated content) in enhanced content modules if available

8. Off-Platform Brand-Building That Feeds Walmart

Walmart doesn't exist in a vacuum. Grow your brand visibility by linking efforts:

- Drive traffic from social media or email to your Walmart storefront
- Promote Walmart-exclusive deals via Instagram, TikTok, or newsletters
- Mention Walmart availability in your off-site ads ("Now available on Walmart.com!")

This builds awareness and **trust** with customers already familiar with your brand elsewhere.

9. Measure Your Brand Growth

Track brand health using Walmart reports and KPIs like:

- Branded search volume

- Storefront traffic
- Repeat purchase rate
- Conversion rates vs. generic competitors
- ROAS on Sponsored Brand Ads

Conclusion

Building a brand on Walmart takes intention and consistency—but it's one of the best long-term strategies for growth. Whether you're just starting or scaling up, think of your brand as more than a logo—it's how customers **remember, trust, and return to you**.

Mastering Walmart SEO & Search Ranking

In this chapter, we'll cover how Walmart's search algorithm works, what you can do to optimize your listings, and how to maintain high visibility over time.

1. Understanding the Walmart Search Algorithm (WES)

Walmart's search engine, known as **WES (Walmart Enhanced Search)**, uses a combination of factors to determine product ranking:

Key Ranking Signals:

- **Relevance** (title, description, keywords)
- **Content quality** (images, attributes)
- **Price competitiveness**

- **In-stock rate & shipping speed**
- **Sales history & performance**
- **Customer reviews and ratings**
- **Fulfillment method (WFS gets preference)**

Walmart prioritizes the **shopper experience**, meaning fast delivery, accurate listings, and trustworthy sellers all influence ranking.

2. Keyword Optimization: Speak the Shopper's Language

Think like your customer. What are they typing into the search bar?

Keyword Placement Best Practices:

- **Product Title:** Include top keywords early (avoid keyword stuffing)
- **Key Features / Bullet Points:** Use mid-to-long-tail keywords naturally
- **Description:** Weave in secondary keywords in a natural, readable flow
- **Backend Attributes:** Always complete Walmart's required and optional item attributes — they feed into search relevance

Keyword Sources:

- Walmart's auto-campaign search term reports
- Amazon keyword tools (many are transferable)
- Competitor listings
- Seasonal trends (e.g., "Mother's Day gifts," "camping gear")

3. Crafting a High-Ranking Product Title

Walmart titles should be **clear, relevant, and keyword-rich**, following this ideal structure:

[Brand] + [Product Type] + [Key Feature] + [Size/Count/Color]

Example:
GlowNest Wireless Earbuds with Charging Case, Bluetooth 5.2, Black

Keep it under **50–75 characters** for best visibility and readability.

4. Product Description & Key Features: Inform + Convert

Key Features:

- Use bullet points
- Include benefits and specifications (e.g., "Water-resistant up to 3ft")
- Highlight differentiators (eco-friendly, made in USA, etc.)

Description:

- Tell your product story clearly
- Focus on clarity + trust-building (shipping info, warranties, brand message)
- Repeat relevant secondary keywords naturally

5. Use Rich Media to Increase Engagement

Listings with rich content **rank better** and **convert more**:

- 4+ high-quality images (including lifestyle & use-case shots)
- Product videos (where supported)
- Enhanced content (A+ content if you're approved)

Visuals improve time-on-page, CTR, and conversion — all of which boost search rank.

6. Pricing & Shipping Influence Rank

Walmart wants to show shoppers the best deal *and* the best experience:

- Keep pricing competitive
- Use **Walmart Fulfillment Services (WFS)** to unlock 2-day shipping badges
- Avoid stockouts or long shipping times — these kill rankings

7. Build Review Volume & Ratings

Customer reviews impact both rankings **and trust**.

Tips to boost reviews:

- Follow up after purchase (if within Walmart's messaging policies)
- Encourage happy customers to leave feedback
- Use review generation tools if available for your product category

Maintain a **4+ star average** for best results.

8. Leverage SEO + Paid Search Together

Paid ads can boost organic rank by:

- Driving traffic to your product pages
- Improving sales velocity
- Increasing relevance through search term performance

Use high-performing **search terms from ad reports** in your SEO strategy.

9. Monitor & Adjust with Analytics

Use these Walmart tools to stay on top of your SEO health:

- **Search Performance Reports** (see where you rank)
- **Item Health Reports** (track missing attributes, content gaps)
- **Keyword performance from ad reports**

Regularly **audit your listings** and keep refining based on performance.

10. SEO Maintenance: Keep It Fresh

Don't "set and forget." Update listings every few months to:

- Reflect seasonal search trends
- Add new keywords
- Refresh images or titles as needed
- Improve underperforming SKUs

Conclusion

Walmart SEO is both an art and a science — it's about aligning your product with what your shoppers are looking for, and making sure your listing is the best option in a sea of search results.

By optimizing keywords, content, price, fulfillment, and reviews, you can climb the rankings and stay visible — which means more clicks, more conversions, and more sales.

Reviews, Ratings, and Customer Service

Reviews, ratings, and customer service have a *huge* influence on conversions for a retail giant like Walmart, especially online. Here's a breakdown of how they impact the customer journey and affect conversion rates:

1. Social Proof Drives Trust

Role in Conversion:

- **Product ratings (stars)** and **written reviews** serve as social proof. When shoppers see high ratings and positive feedback, it builds confidence and encourages them to make a purchase.
- Products with **4+ star ratings** typically have **much higher conversion rates** than unrated or poorly rated items.

Example:
A $20 sneaker on Walmart.com with 4,000+ 5-star reviews often outsells higher-priced competitors with fewer or lower reviews.

2. Customer Reviews Answer Questions

Role in Conversion:

- Reviews often answer key buyer questions that product descriptions don't cover (like fit, sizing, durability).
- **Detailed user feedback** reduces purchase hesitation, especially for apparel, electronics, and home goods.

Conversion Tip:
Walmart highlights "most helpful" or "frequently mentioned" comments to reduce friction and improve trust.

3. Customer Service Impacts Repeat Business

Role in Conversion:

- **Poor customer service = lost future sales.**
- If a shopper has a bad experience with returns, pickups, or online help, they're less likely to come back — even if prices are competitive.
- On the flip side, **resolving issues efficiently** can actually *increase loyalty*.

Example:
Walmart's **free curbside pickup** and **easy returns** policies can be conversion boosters *if* the service is smooth and staff are helpful.

4. Negative Reviews Hurt Conversions – But Not Always

Role in Conversion:

- **Too many 1-star reviews** can tank conversions — especially if the issues mentioned are recent or unresolved.
- But interestingly, a *mix* of reviews (good + bad) can boost authenticity and trust more than only perfect scores.

Conversion Hack:
Walmart often features verified buyer labels and "Top 10 reviewed" filters to guide users toward well-rated products.

5. Order Fulfillment Reviews Matter

Role in Conversion:

- Reviews mentioning **shipping delays, damaged goods,** or **inaccurate listings** discourage buyers.
- Since Walmart sells third-party items too, bad seller ratings can lead to cart abandonment.

Bottom Line:

Strong reviews + responsive service = higher trust = more conversions.
Walmart's eCommerce strategy relies heavily on optimizing these touchpoints. Reviews help convert new customers, and customer service keeps them coming back.

Analyzing Sales Data & Metrics

Analyzing Walmart's sales data and key performance metrics offers valuable insights into the company's operational efficiency, customer behavior, and overall business health. Here's a comprehensive overview:

Key Sales Metrics

1. **Total Sales & Revenue**: Walmart's sales have remained robust, with consistent annual growth. For instance, in 2024, the company reported a 4.1% increase in sales, amounting to $5.25 billion in quarterly earnings.
2. **Sales Velocity**: This metric assesses the rate at which products sell, often measured as Units per Store per Week

(USW) or Dollars per Store per Week ($SW). It helps identify fast-moving products and informs inventory decisions.

3. **Conversion Rate & Average Order Value (AOV)**: These indicators reveal how effectively Walmart turns website visits into purchases and the average amount spent per transaction, respectively.
4. **Customer Lifetime Value (CLTV)**: CLTV estimates the total revenue a customer is expected to generate over their relationship with Walmart, guiding marketing and retention strategies.
5. **Inventory Turnover Rate (ITR)**: This measures how often inventory is sold and replaced over a period, reflecting inventory management efficiency.

Advanced Analytics & Forecasting

Walmart employs sophisticated analytics to enhance sales performance:

- **Big Data Utilization**: The Company leverages big data analytics to understand customer behavior, optimize pricing, and personalize marketing efforts. This includes analyzing social media trends and mobile shopping patterns.
- **Sales Forecasting Models**: Advanced models like LightGBM and ARIMA are used to predict future sales, accounting for factors like seasonality and promotional events. These models help in demand planning and inventory management.

Tools for Sales Analysis

Several tools assist in analyzing Walmart's sales data:

- **Walmart Seller Performance Dashboard**: Provides sellers with metrics on order fulfillment, customer satisfaction, and operational efficiency.
- **KwickMetrics**: Offers real-time sales tracking, customer behavior insights, and advertising analytics, aiding sellers in making informed decisions.
- **Metricalist's Power BI Dashboard**: Provides detailed insights into sales performance, profitability, and trends across various categories and locations.

Customer Behavior Insights

Understanding customer behavior is crucial:

- **Order Patterns**: Walmart has observed a trend towards smaller, more frequent online orders, similar to Amazon's model. This shift indicates changing consumer preferences towards convenience and quick delivery.
- **Basket Analysis**: Analyzing the contents of shopping baskets helps Walmart understand purchasing patterns, enabling personalized promotions and inventory adjustments.

Conclusion

By meticulously analyzing sales data and key performance metrics, Walmart can make informed decisions to enhance customer satisfaction, optimize operations, and drive growth. These insights are vital for maintaining a competitive edge in the dynamic retail landscape.

Avoiding Common Seller Pitfalls

Selling on Walmart Marketplace offers significant opportunities, but it also presents unique challenges. Avoiding common pitfalls is crucial for success. Here's a guide to help you navigate and thrive on the platform:

Common Pitfalls and How to Avoid Them

1. Assuming Walmart Operates Like Amazon

Many sellers transition from Amazon expecting similar operations. However, Walmart has distinct algorithms, customer behaviors, and fulfillment expectations. Strategies effective on Amazon may not yield the same results on Walmart.

Tip: Invest time in understanding Walmart's specific requirements and tailor your approach accordingly.

2. Neglecting the Pro Seller Badge

The Pro Seller Badge enhances visibility and builds customer trust. Ignoring its significance can limit your sales potential.

Tip: Maintain high performance standards to earn and retain this badge, thereby boosting your credibility.

3. Inaccurate or Incomplete Listings

Poorly optimized titles, descriptions, and images can hinder product visibility and sales. Simply copying listings from other platforms without adjustments can be detrimental.

Tip: Craft unique, keyword-rich content tailored to Walmart's SEO guidelines, and ensure high-quality images are used.

4. Pricing Errors

Inconsistent or uncompetitive pricing can lead to suppressed listings or reduced sales.

Tip: Regularly monitor competitor pricing and adjust your strategies to remain competitive while maintaining profitability.

5. **Inventory Mismanagement**

Failing to keep inventory levels updated can result in order cancellations and negative customer experiences.

Tip: Implement robust inventory management systems to ensure accurate stock levels and timely replenishments.

6. *Poor Fulfillment Practices*

Delays in order processing and shipping can harm your seller metrics and customer satisfaction.

Tip: Consider utilizing Walmart Fulfillment Services (WFS) or reliable third-party logistics providers to ensure timely deliveries.

7. *Ignoring Customer Feedback*

Not addressing customer reviews and inquiries can damage your reputation and affect future sales.

Tip: Engage with customer feedback promptly, addressing concerns and implementing improvements based on their suggestions.

8. Underestimating Walmart's Compliance Standards

Non-compliance with Walmart's policies can lead to account suspensions or terminations.

Tip: Stay informed about Walmart's guidelines and ensure all aspects of your operations align with their standards.

Best Practices for Success

- **Optimize Listings:** Use clear, concise titles and descriptions with relevant keywords.
- **Maintain Competitive Pricing:** Regularly review market trends to adjust your pricing strategies.
- **Ensure Accurate Inventory:** Keep your stock levels updated to prevent overselling or stockouts.
- **Prioritize Customer Service:** Respond to inquiries promptly and resolve issues efficiently.
- **Monitor Performance Metrics:** Regularly review your seller dashboard to track key performance indicators and make necessary adjustments.

By proactively addressing these common pitfalls and implementing best practices, you can enhance your performance on Walmart Marketplace and achieve sustained success.

Scaling Your Walmart Business

Scaling your Walmart Marketplace business in 2025 requires a strategic approach that leverages Walmart's tools and services, optimizes your operations, and enhances customer experience. Here's a comprehensive guide to help you expand effectively:

1. Leverage Walmart Fulfillment Services (WFS)

Utilizing WFS can significantly boost your sales by offering:

- **Fast Nationwide Shipping**: WFS provides 2-day shipping, enhancing customer satisfaction.
- **Increased Buy Box Visibility**: Products fulfilled by WFS are more likely to win the Buy Box, leading to higher conversion rates.
- **Cost-Effective Logistics**: Walmart's fulfillment services are approximately 15% cheaper than competitors, offering savings on shipping and storage.

2. Expand Your Product Assortment Strategically

Diversifying your product catalog can attract a broader customer base. Utilize Walmart's Assortment Growth dashboard to:

- **Identify High-Demand Items**: The dashboard recommends best-selling products based on customer demand and category data.
- **Make Informed Decisions**: Leverage insights to add products that align with market trends and customer preferences.

3. Optimize Product Listings for Visibility

Enhance your product listings to improve search rankings and attract more customers:

- **Use Relevant Keywords**: Incorporate keywords that customers are likely to use when searching for products.
- **High-Quality Images and Descriptions**: Provide clear images and detailed descriptions to inform and engage potential buyers.
- **Monitor and Update Listings**: Regularly review and update your listings to reflect current information and optimize performance.

4. Implement Competitive Pricing Strategies

Pricing plays a crucial role in winning the Buy Box and driving sales:

- **Utilize Repricing Tools**: Automated repricing software can help adjust prices in real-time to stay competitive.
- **Balance Price and Profitability**: While competitive pricing is essential, ensure that your prices still allow for a reasonable profit margin.

5. Invest in Walmart Advertising

Boost your product visibility and sales through Walmart's advertising options:

- **Sponsored Products**: Promote your products in search results and product pages to reach more customers.
- **Targeted Campaigns**: Use advertising to focus on specific products, seasons, or customer segments.

6. Enhance Customer Experience

Providing excellent customer service can lead to repeat business and positive reviews:

- **Prompt Communication**: Respond to customer inquiries and issues quickly and professionally.
- **Efficient Fulfillment**: Ensure orders are processed and shipped promptly to meet customer expectations.
- **Manage Reviews**: Monitor and respond to customer reviews to address concerns and build trust.

7. Monitor Performance Metrics

Regularly review your performance to identify areas for improvement:

- **Seller Scorecard**: Use Walmart's Seller Scorecard to track key metrics such as order defect rate, on-time shipping, and customer feedback.
- **Adjust Strategies Accordingly**: Based on performance data, refine your strategies to enhance efficiency and customer satisfaction.

By implementing these strategies, you can effectively scale your Walmart Marketplace business, increase sales, and build a loyal customer base.

Integrating with other Marketplaces

Integrating Walmart Marketplace with other e-commerce platforms like Amazon, eBay, and Shopify is essential for sellers aiming to streamline operations, centralize inventory management, and expand their customer base. Here's a comprehensive guide to help you navigate this process:

Walmart's Integration Methods

Walmart offers several integration options to accommodate different business needs:

1. **Seller Center**: A user-friendly web interface suitable for sellers managing a smaller product catalog.
2. **API Integration**: Ideal for businesses with technical resources, allowing for automation of item setup, order management, pricing, promotions, and inventory updates.
3. **Approved Solution Providers**: Third-party partners that offer services ranging from full-service integration to specialized functions like inventory management or financial services.

Multichannel Integration Strategies

To effectively manage sales across multiple platforms, consider the following strategies:

1. Utilize Walmart's Multichannel Solutions

Walmart's Multichannel Solutions enable sellers to:

- **Consolidate Inventory**: Manage stock across Walmart.com and other sales channels from a centralized system.
- **Leverage Walmart Fulfillment Services (WFS)**: Fulfill orders from various platforms using Walmart's logistics network.
- **Automate Operations**: Integrate with APIs or solution providers to automate order creation, inventory tracking, and returns management.

Note: Participation in Multichannel Solutions requires enrollment in WFS.

2. Partner with Approved Solution Providers

These providers can assist with:

- **Full-Service Integration**: Handling item setup, inventory, order fulfillment, and pricing.
- **Specialized Services**: Focusing on specific areas like content optimization or financial services.

You can manage these partnerships through Walmart's Seller Center or Developer Portal.

3. Employ Third-Party Multichannel Tools

Several platforms offer integrations to synchronize operations across marketplaces:

- **Feedonomics**: Automates product listings and order management across over 300 marketplaces, including Walmart.
- **InfiPlex OMS**: Provides inventory and order management solutions tailored for Walmart sellers.
- **ChannelEngine**: Offers upgraded API integrations to streamline operations and optimize listings on Walmart.
- **Extensiv**: Supports integrations with Walmart Marketplace and other platforms, facilitating order downloads, inventory synchronization, and shipment confirmations.

Fulfillment and Logistics Considerations

When integrating across platforms, efficient fulfillment is crucial:

- **Walmart Fulfillment Services (WFS)**: Utilize WFS to handle storage, shipping, and returns, benefiting from Walmart's logistics network.
- **Multichannel Fulfillment**: Set up items as "Walmart Fulfilled" to enable order fulfillment from various e-commerce sites.
- **Cost Efficiency**: Walmart's fulfillment fees are approximately 15% lower than competitors, offering a cost-effective solution for sellers.

Best Practices for Successful Integration

- **Centralize Inventory Management**: Use integrated systems to maintain accurate stock levels across all platforms.
- **Automate Order Processing**: Implement tools that synchronize orders and tracking information to reduce manual errors.
- **Regularly Update Listings**: Ensure product information is consistent and optimized across all marketplaces.
- **Monitor Performance Metrics**: Track key indicators to identify areas for improvement and adjust strategies accordingly.

By strategically integrating Walmart Marketplace with other e-commerce platforms, you can enhance operational efficiency, expand your reach, and drive growth

Staying Compliant: Policies & Guidelines

Staying compliant with Walmart Marketplace's policies and guidelines is crucial for maintaining your seller account and ensuring a successful business. Here's a comprehensive overview to help you navigate and adhere to Walmart's requirements:

Key Compliance Areas for Walmart Sellers

1. Retailer Agreement & Code of Conduct

All sellers must adhere to the Walmart Marketplace Retailer Agreement and the Seller Code of Conduct. These documents outline expectations for fair pricing, accurate listings, timely fulfillment, and ethical business practices. Non-compliance can lead to account suspension or termination.

2. Product Compliance & Safety

Ensure that all products meet Walmart's safety standards and legal requirements. This includes proper labeling, accurate descriptions, and necessary certifications. Products must not be counterfeit or infringe on intellectual property rights.

3. Prohibited Products Policy

Walmart prohibits the sale of certain items, including but not limited to:

- Counterfeit goods
- Unauthorized replicas
- Certain electronics and health products
- Items sourced through retail arbitrage

Violating this policy can result in product removal or account suspension.

4. Business Information Accuracy

Maintain up-to-date and accurate business information, including legal business name, contact details, and tax identification numbers. Walmart may require periodic verification to comply with laws like the INFORM Consumers Act.

5. Performance Standards

Sellers are expected to meet specific performance metrics:

- **Order Defect Rate**: Low percentage of orders with issues
- **On-Time Delivery Rate**: High percentage of orders delivered on time
- **Valid Tracking Rate**: Providing valid tracking information for shipments
- **Customer Response Time**: Prompt responses to customer inquiries

Regularly monitor your performance dashboard in Seller Center to ensure compliance.

Best Practices for Compliance

- **Stay Informed**: Regularly review Walmart's policies and updates to stay current with any changes.
- **Use Approved Suppliers**: Source products from reputable suppliers to ensure authenticity and compliance.
- **Maintain Clear Communication**: Respond promptly to customer inquiries and resolve issues efficiently.
- **Monitor Listings**: Ensure product listings are accurate, with correct descriptions, images, and pricing.

- **Utilize Walmart Fulfillment Services (WFS)**: Consider using WFS to help meet shipping and delivery standards.

By adhering to these guidelines and maintaining high standards, you can build a trustworthy presence on Walmart Marketplace and foster long-term success.

The Future of Selling on Walmart

The future of selling on Walmart Marketplace in 2025 and beyond is marked by significant growth, technological advancements, and expanded opportunities for sellers. Here's an overview of key trends and strategies to help you thrive:

Explosive Marketplace Growth

- **Rapid Expansion**: Walmart Marketplace has experienced substantial growth, with over 150 million monthly active online shoppers and more than 700 million SKUs offered through third-party sellers.
- **Seller Base Growth**: The platform now hosts over 150,000 sellers, reflecting its increasing popularity among merchants.

AI-Driven Innovation

- **Trend-to-Product Technology**: Walmart utilizes proprietary AI and GenAI tools to swiftly identify and stock trending products, enhancing its competitive edge.

- **Enhanced Customer Experience**: AI-driven personalization improves product recommendations and customer engagement, leading to higher conversion rates.

Global Expansion & Multichannel Selling

- **International Reach**: Sellers can now access markets in Canada, Mexico, and Chile, with plans to enter additional countries, facilitating global business growth.
- **Multichannel Fulfillment**: Walmart's Multichannel Solutions allow sellers to fulfill orders from various platforms using Walmart Fulfillment Services (WFS), streamlining operations.

Enhanced Seller Support

- **Financial Services**: Partnership with JPMorgan Chase accelerates payments to sellers, improving cash flow management.
- **Seller Success Formula**: Walmart offers resources like the Seller Success Formula to guide sellers through best practices and growth strategies.

Diversified Product Categories

- **Luxury Resale Market**: Collaborations with companies like Rebag introduce pre-owned luxury items from brands such as Chanel and Louis Vuitton, attracting a broader customer base.
- **Premium Beauty Segment**: The launch of Premium Beauty on Walmart Marketplace allows exclusive brand representation, catering to upscale consumers.

Strategic Recommendations for Sellers

To capitalize on these developments:

- **Optimize Listings**: Utilize high-quality images, detailed descriptions, and relevant keywords to enhance visibility.
- **Leverage Advertising**: Engage in Walmart's Sponsored Products and Brands ads to increase product exposure.
- **Maintain Compliance**: Adhere to Walmart's policies and performance standards to ensure account health.
- **Expand Globally**: Take advantage of Walmart's international marketplaces to reach new customer segments.

Embracing these trends and strategies will position you for success in Walmart's evolving e-commerce landscape

DISCLAIMER

The Walmart Seller Playbook is an independent publication and is not affiliated with, endorsed by, or sponsored by Walmart Inc. All trademarks and brand names are the property of their respective owners. The information contained in this book is for educational and informational purposes only and does not constitute business, legal, or financial advice.

While every effort has been made to ensure the accuracy and reliability of the information provided, the author and publisher make no representations or warranties of any kind, express or implied, about the completeness, accuracy, suitability, or availability of the content. Readers are advised to conduct their own research and consult with qualified professionals before making any business decisions.

Use of the information in this book is at your own risk. The author and publisher disclaim any liability for direct or indirect losses or damages resulting from the use of the material contained herein.

www.ingramcontent.com/pod-product-compliance
Lightning Source LLC
La Vergne TN
LVHW022355060326
832902LV00022B/4458